MAIN

Kids' Silliest Jokes

Jacqueline Horsfall
Illustrated by Buck Jones

Sterling Publishing Co., Inc.
New York

For Billy, Terry, and Trey–
jokesters all

Library of Congress Cataloging-in-Publication Data Available

Published by Sterling Publishing Company, Inc.
387 Park Avenue South, New York, N.Y. 10016
Text © 2002 by Jacqueline Horsfall
Distributed in Canada by Sterling Publishing
C/o Canadian Manda Group, One Atlantic Avenue, Suite 105
Toronto, Ontario, Canada M6K 3E7
Distributed in Great Britain and Europe by Chris Lloyd
at Orca Book Services, Stanley House, Fleets Lane, Poole BH15 3AJ, England
Distributed in Australia by Capricorn Link (Australia) Pty. Ltd.
P.O. Box 704, Windsor, NSW 2756 Australia

Printed in China
All rights reserved

Sterling ISBN 0-8069-8395-7

Contents

1. Bathtime Belly Laughs   5

2. Shower Slams   14

3. Comic Cleanups   21

4. Jump into Your Jammies   30

5. Bed Springs   36

6. Freaky Fairy Tales   45

7. Moon Madness   51

8. Monsters under the Bed   55

9. Counting Sheep   65

10. Dream Boats and Night Mares   71

11. Rise and Whine   76

12. Knock-Knock Nuttiness   84

Index   94

1. Bathtime Belly Laughs

What do you call an X that just got out of the bathtub?
A clean X.

What would you do if you kept 200 goldfish in the bathtub—and you wanted to take a bath?
Blindfold them.

What happened when Mickey Mouse fell into the bathtub?
He came out squeaky clean.

Why does a bathtub need a cell phone?

Just in case someone rings it up.

What would you say to a skunk that fell into your tub?

"Stink or swim!"

What happened to the skunk that fell into the bathtub?

It stank all the way to the bottom.

If a skunk sprayed you, could you wash it off in the tub?

Let's soap for the best.

What's a ringleader?

The first one into the tub.

Why won't a leopard take a bath with you?

It doesn't want to come out spotless.

Why can't a herd of elephants ever get really clean?

Because they can't take off their trunks.

What fluffy bird calls "whoo, whoo" while you dry off?

A hoot towel.

Why does Mom put corn cobs in the tub?

So you'll wash behind your ears.

Where do sailors take their baths?
In a tubmarine.

Why did the little potato cry in the bathtub?
It got soap in its eyes.

What TV programs should you watch in the bathtub?
Soap operas.

What happened when the rubber duckie fell into the bathtub?
It quacked up.

What do you take when you have a cell phone in the bathroom?

Babble baths.

How do you make a kitchen sink?

Throw it into the bathtub.

How does a bear test its bath water?

With its bear (bare) feet.

What does a goose get when its bath water is too cold?

People-bumps.

Why was the giraffe in the tub for 10 hours?
Its mom told it to wash its neck.

When can't you hold your breath in the bathtub?
When you're holding your washcloth and soap.

Why did Silly Sarah race to the bathroom?
Her boyfriend told her he'd left a ring in the tub.

What disappears when you stand up in the bathtub?
Your lap.

Why did Silly Billy wear slippers in the bathtub?
He heard the bottom was slipper-y.

What did Bigfoot say when he sat on his rubber duckie?
"I've got a crush on you."

Where do fish wash up?
In the bass-tub.

How do you cool down a hot bath?
Dump in a can of chili.

Did you take a bath on Saturday night?
Why? Is one missing?

What kind of toy does the Godfather play with in the tub?

A thug-boat.

How do you make a rubber duckie float?

Put the duckie in a glass and add soda and ice cream.

Why can't you drink apple juice right after a hot bath?

It takes a l-o-n-g time to drink a hot bath.

When can't you take a bath on an airplane?

When the No Soaking sign is on.

What should you do if you find Jaws in the bathtub?

Pull the plug out!

Why did Silly Billy put ice cubes in his father's tub?

Because he likes cold pop.

How many rubber duckies can you put into an empty tub?

One. After that, the tub isn't empty.

What do bumblebees put in the bathtub first?

Their bee-hinds.

What would you be if a shark was in your bathtub?
Chicken of the sea.

What kind of sandwich sinks to the bottom of the tub?
A sub.

Why did Mom test the bath water before putting Silly Billy in?
To prevent son-burn.

Which breed of dogs require daily baths?
Germy Shepherds.

How can you keep your plastic boat from sinking in the bathtub?

Don't hit any icebergs.

What did Mama Mountain tell her children in the bathtub?

"Be sure to wash behind your mountaineers."

Where do good little engines wash themselves?

Behind their engineers.

What happens to a cranberry when you throw it into an icy bath?

It becomes a blue-berry.

How do you make an orange giggle in the tub?

Tickle its navel.

Why did Ms. Centipede spend three months in the tub?

She was shaving her legs.

Did you hear about the two dirty bathtubs that got married?

It was a double-ring ceremony.

What lines did Shakespeare write while soaking in the tub?

"Tub be or not tub be, that is the question."

What happened to Silly Billy when he took a bath in the washing machine?

He got very agitated.

Why did the police officer pack a bar of soap?

The city had a high grime rate.

2. Shower Slams

What does a leopard say in the shower?
"That really hits the spot."

Why did Silly Billy take a shower?
Because the bathtub was too heavy.

What's the best dessert to eat in the shower?
Sponge cake.

What kind of cake makes you gag?
A cake of soap.

Why did Silly Sarah sing in the shower?
She didn't have a bathtub.

Where does a rabbit go for a shampoo?
To a hare-dresser.

How can you keep your hair dry in the shower?
Don't turn on the water.

If someone robbed you in the shower, what would you be?
An eye wetness.

Where does a jogger like to wash up?
Under running water.

What did the faucet say to the shower?
"You're a big drip."

What does it mean if you're muddy, you go home, and you don't have to take a shower?
You're in the wrong house.

Which rock singer really, REALLY needs a shower?
Mud-donna.

SINGING IN THE SHOWER

What Beatles song did the octopus sing in the shower?
"I Wanna Hold Your Hand, Hand, Hand, Hand, Hand, Hand, Hand, Hand."

What does a mummy sing in the shower?
Wrap.

What do fathers sing in the shower?
Pop.

What do goblins sing in the shower?
Rhythm and boos.

What do bumblebees sing in the shower?
BeeBop.

What do angels sing in the shower?
Soul.

What do computer programmers sing in the shower?
Disc-o.

What do trapeze artists sing in the shower?
Swing.

What do steel workers sing in the shower?
Heavy metal.

What kind of opera star sings in the shower?
A soap-rano.

What's a plumber's favorite song?
"Singing in the Drain."

Why did the rabbit wear a shower cap?
It didn't want to get its hare wet.

Why did the shower bar turn red?
Its towel fell off.

What did the minister say when he took a shower?
"Let us spray."

Why did the minister wash himself with a sponge?
He heard it was very hole-y.

What does a newspaper reporter use to dry himself after his shower?
Paper towels.

What's the cleanest store in town?
The soapermarket.

What is the appropriate attire for a wedding in the shower?
A wet suit.

What kind of dog washes its fur in the shower?
A sham-poodle.

Why do basketball players shower after every game?
Because they dribble all over the place.

What animal do you look like in the shower?
A little bear (bare).

Why did the cowboy splash water on the bathroom floor?
Just to horse around.

Did you hear about the soaking wet pregnant woman?
Her friends gave her a shower.

What does a wasp apply after a shower?
Bee-odorant.

What happened to Einstein when he took a shower?

He was brain-washed.

What should you do if someone pulls open the curtain while you're singing in the shower?

Take a bow.

If you held 6 bars of soap in one hand and 10 in the other, what would you have?

Very big hands!

3. Comic Cleanups

If two snakes marry, what will their towels say?
Hiss and Hers.

How did the elephant get into the sewer?
Someone left the seat up.

How did the chimp fix the leaky faucet?
With a monkey wrench.

What did Papa Pig put on his face when he cut himself shaving?
Oink-ment.

Why did Silly Billy stand before the bathroom mirror with his eyes shut?

He wanted to see what he looked like asleep.

What would you do if you broke a tooth while flossing?

Use tooth paste.

What musical instrument is found in the bathroom?

A tuba toothpaste.

How do beetles clean their teeth?

They chew sugar-free buggle gum.

When can't you use a towel to dry off your wet dog?

When you've already used it on your hare.

What makeup did the gorilla apply in the bathroom mirror?

Cover Gorilla.

Which wild animal is a hair stylist?

Bullwinkle the Mousse.

What's a diploma?

When the sink is stopped up, you call diploma.

Why couldn't the police catch the bathroom burglar?
He stepped on the scales and got a weigh.

What did the bathroom rug say to the floor?
"I'm mat about you."

What will happen if you take off all your clothes and stand before a mirror?
If you're in a restaurant, they'll probably call the police.

Why did Silly Billy sign up his aquarium for army duty?
He heard they needed more tanks.

Why did Silly Sarah take trees to the bathroom?
To wash off her dirty palms.

Why did Silly Sarah take a rabbit to the bathroom?
She wanted to blow-dry her hare.

How can you keep your hair from frizzing up in a steamy bathroom?
Turn on the hair conditioner.

Why was the plumber so tired?
He was drained.

What has teeth but can't bite?
A comb.

What has 88 teeth but never brushes them?
A piano.

Why did Silly Sarah decide to go on a diet after she weighed herself?
She was thick and tired of it.

Why did Silly Billy tiptoe past the medicine cabinet?
He didn't want to wake up the sleeping pills.

What did the medicine man see when he stood naked before the bathroom mirror?
His medicine chest.

Why did the moose pose in the bathroom mirror?
To flex his big mooscles.

Why did the male deer smile in the bathroom mirror?
To show off his buck teeth.

How does a robot shave?
With a laser blade.

What's the first thing a dolphin learns at school?
Her A-B-Seas.

Why do dolphins swim in salt water?
Pepper makes them sneeze.

When should you charge your electric toothbrush?
When you can't pay cash.

How do you divide the sea in half?
With a sea saw.

SPLASHERS

How do veterinarians swim laps?
They do the dog paddle.

How do chiropractors swim laps?
They do the back stroke.

How do spiders swim laps?
They do the crawl.

How do caterpillars swim laps?
They do the butterfly.

What did the little lobster get on its math test?
Sea-plus.

How do oysters get ready for work?
They wake up pearly in the morning.

How do eels get out of a muddy seabed?
With 4-eel drive.

Where do jellyfish sleep?
In tent-acles.

Where do sea horses sleep?
Near barn-acles.

Why does Neptune wear a tank top?
To show off his mussels.

What do you call a dandelion floating in the ocean?
Sea weed.

What's a lifeguard's favorite game?
Pool.

Why are astronauts banned from pools?
They make too many splashdowns.

What's another name for submarine pilots?
Deep sea drivers.

Why did Silly Billy run through the sprinkler with his ice cream cone?
He wanted lots of sprinkles on top.

Why did Silly Billy jump into the pool with a bowl of salsa?
He wanted to take a dip.

4. Jump into Your Jammies

What does a slice of toast wear to bed?
Jam-mies.

Where can you lie without being scolded?
In bed.

What do you take off last before getting into bed?
Your feet off the floor.

What would you wear to a graduation ceremony at night school?

A nightcap and nightgown.

Why did Silly Billy wear banana peels on his feet?
He needed a pair of slippers.

How long should a slipper be?
One foot.

What runs around all day and lies under the bed with its tongue hanging out?

A sneaker.

Why does Silly Sarah put rollers in her hair before bed?
So she'll wake curly in the morning.

Why did the radish turn red?
It saw the salad dressing.

What would you do if you trapped an elephant in your pajamas?
Make him take them off!

How did the court know the judge was ready for bed?
He was wearing his robe.

Why did Silly Billy wear a helmet to bed?
So he could crash.

Why did King Arthur wear a T-shirt to bed?
He couldn't find his knight-y.

Why does a T-shirt get larger when you crumple it up?
I don't know, but when you shake it out, you find it in creases.

Why did Silly Billy's mom write TGIF on his slippers?
For "Toes Go In First."

Why is it good to have holes in your underwear?
So you can put your legs through.

How does the Best Man put his kids to bed?
He tux them in.

What famous nurse wore her pajamas all day long?
Florence Nightingown.

What do you have when your head is hot, your foot is cold, and you see spots before your eyes?
A polka-dot sock over your head.

Why did the golfer change his socks?
He had a hole-in-one.

Why did the belt get arrested?
It held up a pair of pants.

Why can't you sleep in your contact lenses?
Your feet would stick out.

What does a germ call his very small robe?
A microbe.

How do birds exercise before they go to bed?
They do worm-ups.

BED WEAR?

What do you wear at a sleepover?
A sleep overcoat.

Why did Silly Sarah wear kangaroo pajamas?
So she could leap into bed.

What does Tony the Tiger wear to bed?
Paw-jamas.

What do lawyers wear to bed?
Their briefs.

What do prize fighters wear to bed?
Boxers.

What do Japanese people wear to bed?
Tea-shirts.

If you look under here, you'll see what most people wear to bed.
Under where?

Why did Silly Billy wear Zorro's cape to bed?

So he could catch some Z's.

How does a chimney sweep carry his pajamas when he travels?

In a soot-case.

5. Bed Springs

What do you call a dog who sleeps on top of your computer?

Browser.

Why can't pickles fall asleep in their jars?

Their covers are on too tight.

Why did Mozart compose symphonies in bed?

He was writing sheet music.

What is a billow?

What you sleep on when you have a bad cold.

What has a waterbed but never rests?

A river.

What do you call a spy who sleeps with a blanket over his head?

An undercover agent.

Why did the yogi sleep on a bed of tacks?

He didn't have time to do his nails.

Why did pioneers sleep in covered wagons?

So they wouldn't have to wait 40 years for a train.

Why did Silly Sally give her sleepover guests a hammer and saw?

She wanted them to make their own beds.

Where would you get the wood to make a bed?

From the slumberyard.

Why did the hockey player stay in bed?

He had the chicken pucks.

BEDHEADS

What kind of bed does Elvis sleep in?
King-size.

What kind of bed does Cleopatra sleep in?
Queen-size.

What kind of bed does a scam artist sleep in?
Bunk.

What kind of bed does a fish sleep in?
Bass-i-net.

What kind of bed do oysters sleep in?
Waterbed.

What kind of bed do baby apes sleep in?
Apri-cots.

What's the difference between a baker and an elephant?
One bakes the bread, the other breaks the bed.

How do we know that most flowers are lazy?

They're always in a bed.

What's the difference between a river and a jogger?

A river can run for miles and never get out of its bed.

Why did the beggar feel like an old bed?

Because everyone kept turning him down.

What does a car get after driving a very long distance?

Tire-d.

Why did Silly Billy want to be reincarnated as a mattress?
So he could lie in bed all day.

Why do you have to go to bed?
Because the bed won't come to you.

Why did Silly Sarah stay in bed all day?
She wanted to conserve energy.

PRIME TIME

What TV programs do cows watch in bed?
Moo-vies.

When do slugs watch TV?
During slime time.

What TV sets do zebras watch?
Black and white.

What movie do tigers watch?
"Claws Encounters of the Furred Kind."

Did you hear the story about the crumpled bed?

It hasn't been made up yet.

Did you hear about the new corduroy pillows?

They're making head lines.

How do you get out of a bedroom with a dresser and a mirror but no windows or doors?

1. Look into the mirror.

2. See what you saw.

3. Take the saw and cut the dresser in half.

4. Two halves make a whole.

5. Climb through the whole.

Why is the sea restless?
It has rocks in its bed.

Why did the ocean roar?
It found crabs in its bed.

How does Mother Nature make her bed?
With sheets of rain and blankets of snow.

Why should you always take a baseball player along if
you want to sleep outdoors?
To pitch the tent.

When is your room like a military dining hall?
When it's a mess.

Why did the computer fall asleep?
It was tired from a hard drive.

What do tired computer programmers do?
They go home and crash.

What do VCR tapes do at night?
They unwind.

How quickly do eggs get ready for bed?
They scramble.

Which mountain is always sleeping?
Mount Everest.

What do you get when you eat crackers in bed?
A crumby night's sleep.

Did you hear about the soldier who bought a
camouflage sleeping bag?
He can't find it.

Why did Silly Billy take money to bed?
In case there was a cover charge.

Why do cowboys sleep on the range?
There isn't enough room on the refrigerator.

How did the wagonmaster hurt himself?
Doing cart wheels.

How did the pancake hurt itself?
Doing backflips.

6. Freaky Fairy Tales

Who is beautiful, gray, and wore big slippers to the ball?

Cinderelephant.

What did Dorothy say while taking a bubble bath in Oz?

"There's no place like foam."

How did Robinson Crusoe survive after his boat sank?

He used a bar of soap and washed himself ashore.

What does Cinderella wear at the beach?
Glass flippers.

Why did Cinderella's tub overflow?
Her rubber duckie turned into a pumpkin.

What's wrong with "rub-a-dub-dub, three men in a tub"?
It isn't very sanitary.

Who does Clark Kent turn into when he takes a
shower?

Soaperman.

Who fell asleep in the bathtub for 100 years?
Rip Van Wrinkled.

What do you call a little bear who never takes a bath?
Winnie-the-Phew!

How do you make bears listen to bedtime stories?
Take away the B, and they're all ears.

Why was Sir Lancelot always so tired?
Because he worked the knight shift.

Why did King Arthur's Round Table have insomnia?
There were a lot of sleepless knights.

What happens to a worm that falls asleep in Sir
Galahad's apple?
It wakes up in the middle of the knight.

Why did Sleeping Beauty sleep so long?
She forgot to leave a wake-up call.

What newspaper do cows read in bed?

The Evening Moos.

What do you call Billy the Kid when he's home in bed with the flu?

A sick shooter.

What bedtime story does Mama Ghost read to her children?

"Ghouldilocks and the Three Bears."

What is your cat's favorite bedtime story?

"Three Blind Mice."

Where do bedtime books sleep?
Under their covers.

What was Camelot famous for?
Its knight life.

Did you hear about the Old Woman Who Lived in a Slipper?
Her shoe was being soled.

What do bakers read to their children at night?
Bread-time stories.

What would you get if you crossed a dentist with a boat?
The Tooth Ferry.

What happened to the boy who slept with his head under his pillow?
The Tooth Fairy took all his teeth!

Why are Tooth Fairies so smart?
They gather a lot of wisdom teeth.

Who writes nursery rhymes while squeezing oranges?
Mother Juice.

Why did Old Mother Hubbard scream when she went to fetch her poor dog a bone?

When she got there, the cupboard was Bear.

Who brings you a bowl of ice cream before she sends you to the ball?

Your Dairy Godmother.

Where does Santa Claus sleep when he's traveling?

In a ho-ho-hotel.

Why was Miss Muffet's spider such a nuisance?

It kept getting in the whey.

What bedtime stories do giants like?

Ones with big words.

What does the Headless Horseman ride?

A nightmare.

What bedtime story does Mama Cow read to her babies?

"Goodnight Moooon."

7. Moon Madness

What's big, bright, and silly?
A fool moon.

Which Olympic high-jumper can jump higher than the moon?
All of them. The moon can't jump.

Why did the astronaut wear a football helmet when he landed on the Moon?
He was making a touchdown.

MAN IN THE MOON

How does the Man in the Moon cut his hair?
Eclipse it.

How does the Man in the Moon wash up?
He takes a meteor shower.

How does the Man in the Moon eat soup?
With a Big Dipper.

How do you know the Man in the Moon likes clear nights?
Because when the clouds disappear, the moon beams.

What does the Man in the Moon get when he plays "Jeopardy"?
The constellation prize.

Why did the Man in the Moon's pants fall down?
He forgot to wear his asteroid belt.

How would you phone the Man in the Moon?
Use E.T. & T.

What snack does the Man in the Moon like?

Space-chips.

How do you know that Saturn has taken a bath in your tub?

It leaves a ring.

How does an astronaut read in bed?

He flicks on a satellight.

How do you get a baby astronaut to go to sleep?

You rock-et.

Why didn't the astronaut eat breakfast?
He wanted to wait until launch time.

If you were abducted in your sleep by aliens, how would they tie you up?
With astro-knots.

What would you take after eating chocolate chip cookies in bed?
A trip to the Milky Way.

What do you call meteorites that don't hit the Earth?
Meteorwrongs.

What's the messiest constellation?
The Big Dripper.

8. Monsters under the Bed

How do you know when there's a dinosaur under your bed?

Your nose touches the ceiling.

How do you know if a dinosaur is in your shower?

You can't close the curtain.

What's the best way to get a demon out of your
bedroom?

Exorcise a lot.

Why do monsters use mouthwash?

They like to gargoyle.

Why do vampires gargle?

So they won't have bat breath.

What happened to the wizard who brushed his teeth
with gunpowder?

He kept shooting his mouth off.

What's the first thing a monster does in the morning?
Wakes up.

What do ghosts put on first thing in the morning?
Their boojeans.

What did the ghost say when it floated through the bedroom wall?
"Pardon me. I'm just passing through."

Why did Sir Galahad take a flashlight to bed?
He was afraid to sleep without a knight light.

What does Bigfoot climb to get to his bedroom?
Mon-stairs.

Why do witches hide under your bed?
They love to play hide-and-shriek.

What do witches ask for when they stop at a hotel?
A broom with a view.

What does a T. Rex do when it sleeps?
Dino-snores.

Who gave King Tut his bath?
His mummy.

BREAKFAST IN BED

What do ghosts order?
Ghosted oats, raisin ghost, and a boo-berry muffin.

What do spiders order?
Scrambled legs, whole wheat ghost, and apple spider.

What do scarecrows order?
Straw-berries, brain muffin, and flapjack-o-lanterns.

What do witches order?
Sand-witch spread with black cats-up, deviled eggs, and low-fat I scream.

What do ghouls order?
Stir-fright vegetables, screamed corn, and scare-ot cake.

What do vampires order?
Mushroom bites, artichoke hearts with screamy yogurt dressing, T-bone stakes, and neck-tarines.

What does Bigfoot order?
Smashed potatoes and squash.

What's hairy, fanged, and 4-feet tall?
An 8-foot werewolf taking a bow.

Why did Dracula walk around in his pajamas?
Because he didn't own a bat robe.

Why was the little ghost trapped in the linen closet?
Its mom folded its sheet.

Why was Dracula so sleepy?
He kept biting people with tired blood.

Why does Frankenstein look so stiff when he walks?
His mom starched his underwear.

What do you say to quiet a ghost under your bed?
"Please don't spook until you're spooken to."

Why did the baby ghost wear a pillowcase?
The sheet was too big.

What does the Invisible Man rub into his face before he retires?
Vanishing Cream.

What wears an eyepatch and robs ships at night?
A vampirate.

Why did the skeleton shoo the dog off his bed?
Because he's such a bonehead.

What did Mama Ghost say to her children when they got in the car?
"Fasten your sheetbelts."

What would you get if Bambi met a ghost under your bed?
Bamboo.

Why does Dracula want to meet your family?
He really likes the necks of kin.

What do you call a gorilla wearing headphones?
Anything. He can't hear you.

Where do monsters sleep on Halloween?
At the Howliday Inn.

Why is the Blob always the last one to bed?
Because when you ooze, you lose.

Why didn't the skeleton go to the pajama party?
She had no body to go with.

What do witches use after they've blow-dried their hair?

Scare-spray.

What do you say to a skeleton before it eats breakfast?

"Bone appetit!"

What does Dracula read each morning before breakfast?

His horror-scope.

Why was E.T. the Extraterrestrial late for the sleepover?

He had to phone home.

What do witches do after a sleepover?
They go home for a spell.

What do you get when a giant steps on your room?
A mush-room.

How did the dragon burn his hair?
He sneezed into his pillow.

What boy wizard magically grew a beard each night?
Hairy Potter.

Why did the ghost hire a maid?
To change his sheets every day.

Why did the baby ghost cry himself to sleep?
He had a boo-boo.

How does a witch know what time to get up?
She looks at her witch watch.

What time would it be if 10 ghouls chased you in your sleep?
Ten after one.

What's a 500-pound vampire hovering over your bed?
A huge pain in the neck.

Why couldn't the Swamp Thing get out of the tub?

It got bogged down.

Why do witches think they're funny?

Every time they look into the bathroom mirror, it cracks up.

What should you say when you meet a ghost in your bedroom?

"How do you boo?"

Where does a werewolf like to hide?

In your claws-it.

Why did the werewolf take a bite out of the tightrope walker?

It wanted to have a well-balanced diet.

What did the little zombie say to her father before she went to bed?

"Goodnight, Dead-y."

9. Counting Sheep

Why did the sheep get pulled over by a state trooper?
They took a ewe turn.

Where do the sheep go after you count them?
To the baaaathroom.

How did Mary feel about her little lamb's insomnia?
She wasn't going to lose any sheep over it.

If a lamb slipped in the shower, how would you get
it to the hospital?
By lambulance.

Why is it easier to count cows than sheep?
You can use a cowculator.

What would you get if you crossed a sheep and a monkey?
A baa-boon.

What do sheep do when they go out on a date at night?
A little star-grazing.

What do lambs do if they can't fly?
Go by spacesheep.

What do you call the place where they shear sheep?
A baa-baa shop.

Why couldn't the little lamb get up in the morning?
It was still asheep.

Why is it hard to say your prayers with a goat around?
It keeps butting in.

What toys do baby snakes take to bed?
Their rattles.

What did the whale do when his mom made him go to bed early?

He blubbered.

What time is it when an elephant climbs into your bed?

Time to get a new bed.

Why did Silly Billy put a toad in his sister's bed?

He couldn't find a spider.

How do you get rid of bedbugs?

Make them sleep on the sofa.

What prayer do cows say at bedtime?
  "Do unto udders."

Why can't snakes say their prayers before bed?
  They don't have any knees.

What does Mama Snake give her babies before they go to sleep?
  Hugs and hisses.

What did the monkey say when his tail got caught in the bedroom fan?
  "It won't be long now."

Why did Mama Duck scold her goslings?
  For eating quackers in bed.

Why did Silly Billy put a roll of film under his pillow?
  To see if anything developed.

Why did Silly Sarah blow up a paper bag?
  She wanted to hit the sack.

Why did the orange fall asleep during dinner?
  It ran out of juice.

Do you fall asleep on your left side or your right?

Both. All of you goes to sleep at the same time.

What animal pouts when it has to go to bed?

A whinoceros.

What did the sleeping dog say when he fell off the couch?

"W-oof!"

Who stays with young squids when their parents go out?

Baby-squidders.

Why shouldn't you put a four-leaf clover under your pillow?

You don't want to press your luck.

Why couldn't the pony sing himself a lullaby?
He was a little hoarse.

What happened when Ms. Owl got a sore throat?
She didn't give a hoot.

10. Dream Boats and Night Mares

Why did Silly Sarah take a bale of hay to bed with her?
To feed her night mare.

Why can't computers remember their dreams?
They're always losing their memories.

How do you know Kermit the Frog had a bad dream?
He toad you so.

What does Mama Pheasant say when she kisses her children goodnight?

"Pheasant dreams."

Where did Cinderella Spaghetti dream she was going?
To the Meat Ball.

Why did Silly Sarah take sugar to bed?
To have sweet dreams.

SWEET DREAMS

What movie do pigs dream about?
"Jurassic Pork."

Which rock star do bumblebees dream about?
Sting.

Which rock star does Sleeping Beauty dream about?
Prince.

What movie star do travel agents dream about?
Tom Cruise.

Which rock group do exterminators dream about?
The Beatles.

What late-night host do post office workers dream about?
David Letter-man.

What do waiters dream about?
Sirloin tips.

What confusing dream did the Egyptian girl have?
She dreamed her daddy was a mummy.

Why did the banana wear snore-strips on his nose?
He didn't want to wake up the rest of the bunch.

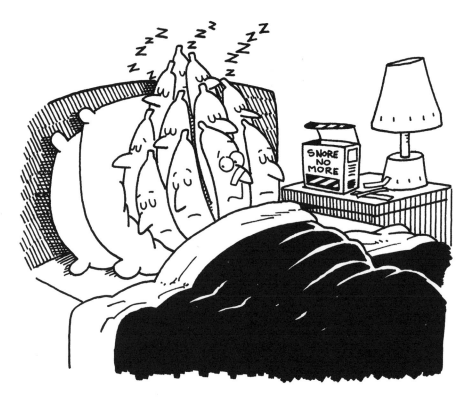

How much does the Sandman charge you if you fall
asleep on the beach?
A sand-dollar.

Why did Silly Sarah keep an exercycle in her
bedroom?
She was tired of walking in her sleep.

How does an ESP expert send his dreams?
With a sixth-sense stamp.

How do pigs communicate their dreams?
In swine language.

Why did the baby goat cry when he had a bad dream?
Because he was just a little kid.

Where do hockey players dream of playing?
At the Empire Skate Building.

What is a spider's favorite dream?
Being on the Worldwide Web.

11. Rise and Whine

Why was the crab crabby when he woke up?
The sea snore kept him up all night.

Why was the broom late?
It overswept.

Why did the worm oversleep?
So it wouldn't get caught by the early bird.

Why did Silly Billy fall asleep at his desk?
  He'd been up since the crack of yawn.

Why did Silly Sarah take yeast and furniture polish to bed?
  So she'd rise and shine.

Why did Silly Billy's father leave the muffler shop?
  He got too exhausted.

Why did the employee fall asleep at work?
  His boss told him he should retire early.

What's the difference between coffee and an elephant?
  Elephants don't keep you up all night.

What did Obi-Wan Kenobi say to Luke Skywalker at breakfast?
  Use the fork, Luke.

What did the bread do when it woke up?
  Loafed around.

Why did the banana apply sunscreen when the sun came up?
  Because it peels.

BREAK YOUR FAST

What does the washing machine eat for breakfast?
Soap flakes.

What does Kermit the Frog eat for breakfast?
Green eggs and ham.

What do cheerleaders eat for breakfast?
Cheer-ee-ohs!

What do race car drivers eat for breakfast?
Fast food.

What do cannibals eat for breakfast?
Buttered host.

What do beavers eat for breakfast?
Oakmeal.

What do cats eat for breakfast?
Mice Krispies.

What do rabbits eat for breakfast?
Cinnamon bun-nies.

What do dogs eat for breakfast?
  Pooched eggs and barkon.

What do canaries eat for breakfast?
  Cream of tweet.

What do comedians eat for breakfast?
  Corny flakes.

What do sharks eat for breakfast?
  Captain Crunch.

What does Humpty Dumpty eat for breakfast?
  Egg drop soup.

What has hands but never washes them?
A clock.

What timepiece leaps tall buildings in a single bound?
Clock Kent.

What wakes you up when it gets scared ?
An alarmed clock.

What goes "ring, ring" every morning at the wrong time?
A false alarm clock.

Why did the pilot sit on her alarm clock?
She wanted to be on time.

What happened when the dog swallowed an alarm clock?
It got a lot of ticks.

Why shouldn't you throw your alarm clock across the room?
Because it's a waste of time.

How do you know when your alarm clock is hungry?
It goes back for seconds.

Why did the alarm clock get sick?
It was run down.

TIME TO GET UP

What time does a shark get up?
Ate o'clock.

What time does a gambler get up?
Twenty to one.

What time do twins get up?
Two o'clock.

What time does a doctor get up?
Sicks o'clock.

What time does a dentist get up?
Tooth hurty.

What time does an oak get up?
Tree o'clock.

What time does a tennis player get up?
Ten-ish.

What time does a duck get up?
At the quack of dawn.

How do trees feel after a good night's sleep?
Re-leafed.

How do bees get to school in the morning?
On the school buzz.

Why did Silly Sarah sleep on the counter?
So she could see the sun rise and the kitchen sink.

12. Knock-Knock Nuttiness

Knock-knock.
   Who's there?
Juicy.
   Juicy who?
Juicy any ghosts
under my bed?

Knock-knock.
   Who's there?
Dewey.
   Dewey who?
Dewey really have to go
to bed right now?

Knock-knock.
Who's there?
Pasture.
Pasture who?
Pasture bedtime, isn't it?

Knock-knock.
Who's there?
Sherwood.
Sherwood who?
Sherwood like to
get some sleep!

Knock-knock.
Who's there?
Tom Sawyer.
Tom Sawyer who?
Tom Sawyer underwear.

Knock-knock.
Who's there?
Wilma.
Wilma who?
Wilma hot chocolate
be ready soon?

Knock-knock.
Who's there?
Duncan.
Duncan who?
Duncan donuts in
my hot chocolate
makes them soggy.

Knock-knock.
Who's there?
Culver.
Culver who?
Culver me up, I'm freezing!

Knock-knock.

Who's there?

Philip.

Philip who?

Philip the tub a little higher, please.

Knock-knock.

Who's there?

Owl.

Owl who?

Owl read you a bedtime story if you read me one.

Knock-knock.
  Who's there?
Jillian.
  Jillian who?
Jillian bucks I can water ski in
the bathtub.

Knock-knock.
  Who's there?
Honeydew.
  Honeydew who?
Honeydew you like your shower hot or cold?

Knock-knock.
  Who's there?   Knock-knock.
Beehive.   Who's there?
  Beehive who?   Kleenex.
Beehive yourself!   Kleenex who?
                          Kleenex look better
                          than dirty necks.

Knock-knock.
  Who's there?
Jimmy.
  Jimmy who?
Jimmy a little kiss before you go to bed.

Knock-knock.

Who's there?

Honeycomb.

Honeycomb who?

Honeycomb your hair when you get out of the shower.

Knock-knock.

Who's there?

Alaska.

Alaska who?

Alaska if I have to take a bath again tomorrow.

Knock-knock.

Who's there?

Myth.

Myth who?

Myth my two fwont teetfh.

Knock-knock.

Who's there?

Eileen.

Eileen who?

Eileen over to
paint my toenails.

Knock-knock.

　Who's there?

Goliath.

　Goliath who?

Goliath down, you looketh tired.

Knock-knock.

　Who's there?

Canoe.

　Canoe who?

Canoe hang up my
towels for me?

Knock-knock.

　Who's there?

Orange juice.

　Orange juice who?

Orange juice sorry you put the cat in the tub?

Knock-knock.

　Who's there?

Oliver.

　Oliver who?

Oliver body will be clean if she scrubs with a washcloth.

Knock-knock.
Who's there?
Tuba.
Tuba who?
Tuba toothpaste
and some floss, and
my teeth sparkle.

Knock-knock.
Who's there?
Omelet.
Omelet who?
Omelet smarter
than I look.

Knock-knock.
Who's there?
Pizza.
Pizza who?
Pizza real clean guy when
he gets out of the shower.

Knock-knock.
Who's there?
Norma Lee.
Norma Lee who?
Norma Lee I don't take
two showers in one day.

Knock-knock.

Who's there?

Anita.

Anita who?

Anita bath, BAD!

Knock-knock.

Who's there?

Ben.

Ben who?

Ben dover and dry your toes.

Knock-knock.

Who's there?

Icon.

Icon who?

Icon shower faster than you can.

Knock-knock.

Who's there?

Charlotte.

Charlotte who?

Charlotte of bubbles in this tub tonight.

Knock-knock.

Who's there?

Unawares.

Unawares who?

Unawares what you put on first every morning.

Knock-knock.

Who's there?

Wendy.

Wendy who?

Wendy soap's all gone, you can't wash yourself.

Knock-knock.

Who's there?

Senior.

Senior who?

Senior rubber duckie lately?

Knock-knock.

Who's there?

Wooden.

Wooden who?

Wooden you like to sleep over?

Knock-knock.

Who's there?

Thesis.

Thesis who?

Thesis the coldest bed I've ever slept in.

Knock-knock.

Who's there?

Ammonia.

Ammonia who?

Ammonia little kid who can't reach the sink.

Knock-knock.

Who's there?

Zoo.

Zoo who?

Zoo long, I'm outta here!

Index

Airplane, 10
Alaska, 88
Aliens, 54
Ammonia, 93
Angels, 17
Anita, 91
Apes, 38
Aquarium, 23
Arthur, King, 32
Astronaut, 29, 51, 53, 54
Baker, 38
Bambi, 60
Banana, 74, 77
Baseball player, 42
Basketball players, 19
Bath, 5-13, 47, 53, 57, 88, 91
Bathtub, 5-13, 46, 47, 64, 86, 87, 89, 91
Beach, 46
Bear, 8, 19, 47, 50
Beard, 63
Beatles, 73; song, 16
Bed wear, 34
Bed, 30-44, 54, 55, 67, 92; bugs, 56, 67; room, 41
Bedtime, 85; story, 48, 49, 50, 86
Beehive, 87
Bees, 83; see Bumblebees
Beetles, 22
Beggar, 39
Belt, 33, 52
Ben, 91
Best Man, 33
Big Dipper, 52
Bigfoot, 9, 57, 58
Billow, 37
Billy the Kid, 48
Birds, 6, 33
Blob, 61

Boat, 12, 49
Bakers, 38, 49
Books, 49
Bread, 38, 77
Breakfast, 54, 78-79; in bed, 58
Breath, 9
Broom, 57, 76
Bullwinkle, 22
Bumblebees, 10, 17, 73
Burglar, 23
Cake, 14
Camelot, 49
Camouflage, 43
Canaries, 79
Canoe, 89
Car, 39
Cat, 48, 89
Caterpillars, 27
Cell phone, 6, 8
Centipede, 13
Ceremony, marriage, 13, 19
Charlotte, 91
Chili, 9
Chimney sweep, 35
Chimp, 21
Chiropractors, 27
Cinderella, 45, 46, 72
Clark Kent, 47
Cleanups, 21-29
Cleopatra, 38
Clock, 80-81
Clothing, 30-35
Clover, four leaf, 70
Coffee, 77
Cold, 37
Comb, 25
Computer, 36, 42, 71; programmers, 17, 42
Constellation, 54
Contact lenses, 33
Cookies, 54
Corn cobs, 6

Cover charge, 43
Covered wagons, 37
Cowboy, 19, 44
Cows, 40, 48, 50, 66
Crabs, 42, 76
Crackers, 43
Cranberry, 12
Crime, 13
Cruise, Tom, 73
Culver, 85
Dandelion, 28
Deer, 25
Demon, 56
Dentist, 49, 82
Dessert, 14
Dewey, 84
Diet, 25
Dinosaur, 55
Diploma, 22
Doctor, 82
Dog, 11, 19, 22, 36, 69, 81
Dolphin, 26
Dracula, 59, 61, 62
Dragon, 63
Dreams, 71-75
Duck, 68, 82
Duncan, 85
E.T., 52, 62
Eels, 27
Eggs, 42
Eileen, 88
Einstein, 20
Elephant, 6, 21, 31, 38, 45, 67, 77
Elvis, 38
Employee, 77
Engines, 12
ESP expert, 75
Exercycle, 74
Fairy Godmother, 50
Fairy tales, 45-50
Fathers, 17
Feet, 30

Film, 68
Fish, 9, 38
Floss, 90
Flossing, 22
Flowers, 39
Flu, 48
Frankenstein, 60
Furniture polish, 77
Galahad, Sir, 47, 57
Gambler, 82
Gargoyle, 56
Germ, 33
Ghosts, 48, 57, 58, 59,
  60, 63, 64, 84
Ghouls, 58, 63
Giants, 50, 63
Giraffe, 9
Goat, 66, 75
Goblins, 17
Godfather, 10
Goldfish, 5
Golfer, 33
Goliath, 89
Goose, 8
Gorilla, 22, 61
Graduation, 31
Gunpowder, 56
Hair, 15, 18, 24, 31, 52,
  62, 63, 88; stylist, 22
Halloween, 61
Hay, 71
Headless Horseman,
  50
Helmet, 32, 51
High-jumper, 51
Hockey players, 37, 75
Honeycomb, 88
Honeydew, 87
Hot chocolate, 85
Humpty Dumpty, 79
Ice cubes, 10
Icon, 91
Insomnia, 65
Invisible Man, 60
Japanese people, 34
Jaws, 10
Jellyfish, 27
Jillian, 87
Jimmy, 87

Jogger, 15, 39
Judge, 31
Kermit the Frog, 71
King Arthur, 32
King Tut, 57
Kiss, 87
Kleenex, 87
Knight, 47
Knock-knocks, 84-93
Lamb, 65, 66
Lancelot, 47
Lap, 9
Lawyers, 34
Leopard, 6, 14
Letterman, David, 73
Lifeguard, 28
Lobster, 27
Luke Skywalker, 77
Lullaby, 70
Maid, 63
Man in the moon, 52-
  53
Mattress, 40
Medicine chest, 25
Mess, 42
Meteor shower, 52
Meteorites, 54
Mickey Mouse, 5
Milky Way, 54
Minister, 18
Mirror, 22, 23
Money, 43
Monkey, 66, 68
Monsters, 55-64
Moon, 51-54
Moose, 25
Mother Nature, 42
Mountain, 12, 43
Mouthwash, 56
Movie, 73; star, 73
Movies, 40
Mozart, 36
Muffet, Miss, 50
Muffler shop, 77
Mummy, 16, 57, 73
Music, 36
Myth, 88
Necks, 61, 87
Neptune, 28

Newspaper, 48;
  reporter, 18
Nightmare, 50, 71
Norma Lee, 90
Nurse, 33
Nursery rhymes, 49
Oak, 82
Obi-Wan Kenobi, 77
Ocean, 42
Old Mother Hubbard,
  50
Oliver, 89
Omelet, 90
Opera star, 17
Orange, 13, 49, 68;
  juice, 89
Owl, 70, 86
Oysters, 27, 38
Oz, 45
Pajama party, 61
Pajamas, 31, 33, 34, 35,
  59
Palms, 24
Pancake, 44
Pants, 52
Paper bag, 68
Pheasant, 72
Philip, 86
Phone, 52
Piano, 25
Pickles, 36
Pigs, 73, 75
Pillowcase, 60
Pillows, 41
Pills, 25
Pioneers, 37
Pirate, 60
Pizza, 90
Plumber, 17, 24
Pony, 70
Pool, 28, 29
Post office workers, 73
Potato, 7
Potter, Hairy, 63
Prayers, 68
Prince, 73
Prize fighters, 34
Pumpkin, 46
Rabbits, 15, 18, 24, 78

Radish, 31
Restaurant, 23
Retiring, 77
Ring, 9
Ringleader, 6
Rip Van Winkle, 47
River, 37, 39
Robbery, 15
Robe, 33
Robinson Crusoe, 45
Robot, 25
Rock: group, 73; singer, 15; star, 73
Rocks, 42
Rubber duckie, 7, 9, 10, 46, 92
Rug, 23
Sailors, 7
Salsa, 29
Sandman, 74
Sandwich, 11
Santa Claus, 50
Satellite, 53
Saturn, 53
Sawyer, Tom, 85
Scam artist, 38
Scarecrows, 58
Sea, 26, 42; horses, 28
Seatbelts, 60
Senior, 92
Shakespeare, 13
Shampoo, 15, 19
Shark, 11, 82
Shave, 25
Shaving, 21
Sheep, 65, 66
Sherwood, 85
Shoe, 49
Shower, 55, 87, 88, 90, 91
Showers, 14-20
Singer, 15
Singing in the shower, 15, 16-17, 20
Sink, 8, 83, 93
Skeleton, 60, 61, 62

Skunk, 6
Sleep, 57, 69
Sleeping, 77-83; bag, 43; Beauty, 47, 73; pills, 25
Sleepover, 37, 62, 63
Slippers, 9, 31, 32, 49
Slugs, 40
Snack, 53
Snakes, 21, 68; baby, 66
Sneaker, 31
Soap, 6, 7, 13, 14, 45, 92; operas, 7
Sock, 33
Soup, 52
Spiders, 27, 50, 58, 67, 75
Sponge, 18
Sprinkler, 29
Spy, 37
Squids, 69
Steel workers, 17
Sting, 73
Store, 19
Sub, 11
Submarine pilots, 29
Sunscreen, 77
Swamp Thing, 64
Swimming, 27
Tail, 68
Teeth, 25, 88
Tennis player, 82
Tent, 42
TGIF, 32
Thesis, 92
Ticks, 81
Tigers, 34, 40
Tightrope walker, 64
Time, 80-82
Toad, 67
Toast, 30
Toenails, 88
Tooth, 22; brush, electric, 26; Fairy, 49
Toothpaste, 22, 90

Towel, 6, 18, 22, 89
Trapeze artists, 17
Trees, 24, 83
T-shirt, 32
Tub, 5-13, 46, 86, 89, 91
Tuba, 22, 90
Tux, 33
TV programs, 7, 40
Twins, 82
Tyrannosaurus Rex, 57
Underwear, 33, 34, 60, 92
Vampires, 56, 58, 60, 63
VCR tapes, 42
Veterinarians, 27
Wagonmaster, 44
Wagons, covered, 37
Waiters, 73
Wake-up call, 47
Waking up, 76-83
Washing machine, 13
Wasp, 19
Water ski, 87
Waterbed, 37
Wedding, 19
Wendy, 92
Werewolf, 59, 64
Wet suit, 19
Whale, 67
Wilma, 85
Witches, 57, 58, 62, 63, 64
Wizard, 56
Wood, 37
Wooden, 92
Worm, 47, 76
X, 5
Yeast, 77
Yogi, 37
Zebras, 40
Zombie, 64
Zoo, 93
Zorro, 35